# WALL STREET SPECULATION:

## ITS TRICKS AND ITS TRAGEDIES

# FRANKLIN C. KEYES

COSIMO CLASSICS

NEW YORK

Cosimo, P.O. Box 416
Old Chelsea Station
New York, NY 10113-0416

or visit our website at:
www.cosimobooks.com

*Wall Street Speculation: Its Tricks and Its Tregedies* was originally published by Fraser Publishing in 1904.

**Library of Congress Cataloging-in-Publication Data**
A catalog record for this book is available from the Library of Congress

Cover design by www.wiselephant.com

ISBN: 1-59605-486-7

# WALL STREET SPECULATION

# Wall Street Speculation.

## ITS TRICKS AND ITS TRAGEDIES.

### PART I—ITS TRICKS.

### I.

W ALL Street speculation is the most stupendous game known to the world of chance; as compared with it, the game at Monte Carlo pales into utter insignificance; in no other game are the stakes so high, is success so transitory and failure so overwhelming. It is a game in which the wealth of Crœsus changes hands in a single hour, a game in which a few manipulators behind the scenes pile up millions on top of more millions year after year; but in which the vast majority of the outside public, who tamper with it, go to financial and often to physical and moral ruin.

Many who are unacquainted with Wall Street methods, regard speculation in stocks, on a margin, as legitimate business; this however is an error, which we may as well acknowledge first as last; it is, as I say, a game, run by Wall Street's millionaires and multimillionaires, who since the organization of the Stock Exchange have succeeded in filching from the pockets of the general public, without giving any equivalent whatever, untold millions.

The public's annual average of loss to Wall Street has usually been estimated in former years, at $100,-000,000 per annum; but owing to the more recent enterprising methods of the " Street," in manipulating the game, this estimate is now far too small, as we shall see.

Beginning with September, 1902, we witnessed for over a year thereafter an almost continuous decline in the stock market, a decline manipulated by the Standard Oil party and largely superinduced and made possible by the dishonest organization and over-capitalization of trust properties by the so-called " great captains of industry." These corporations were not only overcapitalized, until the ciphers ran out, but were bled of vast sums, generally by their organizers, for underwriting their securities or, in other words, for unloading their stocks and bonds, at inflated prices, upon the unsuspecting public.

On this decline, the shrinkage in market value of stocks and bonds on the various exchanges amounted to the unprecedented sum of approximately three billion dollars; and the proportion of this vast amount fleeced from the public in cold cash is so large, that the public's annual average of loss is now certainly far beyond the one hundred million dollar mark.

The general public seldom have any opportunity to become familiar with the inside workings of Wall

Street speculation, as it really is, except through an expensive personal experience; but by the time most people have learned enough through personal experience to make money in Wall Street, their experience is all the capital that they have left, and this alone makes rather a light margin, with which to operate in stocks.

Those who have had experience and lost, invariably keep the lamentable matter as quiet as possible. To disclose their losses would injure their credit and their business standing and would be a reflection upon their sagacity, so you do not learn anything from them. Those who have been fortunate enough to make money, also keep perfectly quiet; they prefer to have you think that their wealth was accumulated in some legitimate business, and so you learn nothing from them.

A candid statement of the facts, therefore, and an honest disclosure of the wiles employed in Wall Street to ensnare the general public would not seem uncalled for. This will appear the more expedient, when we consider the demoralizing and ruinous effects of stock gambling upon the country at large, when we recall the prosperous business houses forced to the wall by '' outside speculation '' or by the embezzlements of speculating clerks, when we remember the banking institutions wrecked by speculating officials, and the many honest men who have been converted into thieves and forgers and driven to despair and suicide through their losses in Wall Street.

## II.

THERE is of course a legitimate side of Wall
Street; it is here that great enterprises may be
honestly financed; it is here that the surplus money
of the country, unemployed in general business, may
find a quick and often a profitable investment, in railroad and industrial stocks and bonds; it is through
Wall Street that public bond issues have been quickly
floated to relieve the Federal government, in times of
financial distress.   The legitimate side of Wall Street,
therefore, is nearly as great a necessity, in our financial system, as the United States Treasury; it serves
as a propelling center, through which the financial life
blood of the nation courses.

It is not this side of Wall Street, however, that we
shall consider here, but the speculative side, in which
too many of the general public are more or less interested and infatuated; the side that wastes its life, in
trying to chase the flying fractions up and down the
fluctuations of the market; the side that buys stocks,
not outright for investment but on margin for speculation; the side, as some one has expressed it, that tries
to take a shoestring and run it into a shoe store.

Some great fortunes, we must admit, have been
made in stock speculation; but this is possible only for
a few insiders, and not for the general public; their
fortunes are lost, not made here.   With the public,

money acquired in marginal transactions, if at all, is sooner or later lost in the same way, and generally much more with it. Brokers' books show that only about one speculator in ten ever makes anything, the other nine lose, and of this one-tenth who make, not one in ten keeps his profits.

You have, therefore, about one chance in a hundred to beat the game. Now wouldn't you consider that rather desperate gambling? It certainly is and the reason why the public ever become involved in stock speculation is because, at the start, they know nothing about it.

Jay Gould, in the management, wrecking and development of great railroad properties, rigged the stock market up and down, to his vast profit; but as he was in a position, through his connection with these corporations, to virtually control the market price of their stocks, with him it was scarcely a speculation at all, but rather, a certainty; and bear in mind that what he alone made, in stock speculation, pure and simple, the general public had to lose, since he won fortune from the ruin of thousands.

What may be said of Gould, as to the element of chance, may also be said of the "Standard Oil crowd" to-day, for with this powerful faction, the most powerful and dangerous ever in Wall Street, stock speculation is much more of a certainty than it could be with Jay Gould.

## III.

IF there was ever an *Ignis fatuus*, a delusion and a snare, the speculative side of Wall Street is one. If the speculator, by any chance, should at first blunder into making money rapidly, as is sometimes the case, his days are numbered; for this first success is, almost surely, the precursor of his untimely fall; and the larger his first profits, the greater will be the shock of that fall.

There can be nothing more stimulating, more exhilarating, more intoxicating, than these first successes in Wall Street speculation, seeming to open up a smooth and easy path to great wealth, power and happiness. With the coming of these first profits, the speculator begins to dream dreams and see visions. What appears to him, in these dreams, naturally depends upon his temperament and tastes, his early education and environment.

One man, perhaps, sees a fine stable of horses and the excitement and enthusiasm of the race course; he sees his favorites win the victory and hears the shouts of excited thousands; another man dreams of abundant leisure and freedom from distracting care; he sees an easy chair before a cheerful fire, and surrounding him his splendid library, the choice literature of all the ages, through which he may commune with the great souls of earth; another dreams himself the owner of a grand mansion, standing amid stately parks; he sees its velvet lawns, its verdant shrubbery and beautiful flowers, he sees its walls hung with the rich tapestries of the East and with the rare paintings of genius, he hears strains of sweet music and the laughter of convivial feasts — here shall be boundless hospitality and here shall be endless delight; another sees a panorama of travel in foreign lands, and a season of pleasure and profit in the great capitals of Europe; another dreams of a happy home, with all the comforts and luxuries of life, beautiful children, a loving wife, radiant with contentment and joy.

These are some of the dreams, these are some of the illusions which rainbow-like appear before the mental vision of the successful Wall Street speculator; elevated into the seventh heaven, when his fortune turns, as turn it will, great and overwhelming is his fall — the bullet hole in the temple, the acid-stained lips, the stiff and lifeless body, lifted from the river, tell the sad tale of disappointment and despair.

## IV.

TO make money by speculation in stocks, on margin, looks to the uninitiated more easy even than the proverbial inexertion of "rolling off a log." It is the opinion of the inexperienced that all one has to do is to send an order down to Wall Street in the morning, and along toward evening a van will back up to his front door and unload about a billion dollars in gold bullion. Such is the delusion.

Wall Street, however, is dominated by some of the brainiest and shrewdest men in the country, natural-born sharpers and schemers, and before the average man can get the better of them, except through the merest chance, he will have to eat brain food for a long time.

Stock speculation, as I say, looks easy; the stocks can go only two ways, either up or down — you do not have to spend any time looking out for their dodging sideways — all that you have to do is to buy when they are low, and sell when they are high. But after the novice has tried it awhile, for some mysterious reason he changes his mind completely about its being easy and telegraphs for money to get home. He is forced to conclude that there is no more difficult way to make money, and no easier or surer way to lose it. He finds, although he cannot explain it or account for it, that somehow every time he buys stocks they go down, and every time he sells them short for a decline, they go up.

Occasionally, perhaps, he really gets his mind on the right side of the market, but at these times he never has the courage of his convictions to invest; he most likely is dissuaded by some one's opinion or casual remark, and so he stands by and looks on, torn and exasperated with always losing his opportunity, which is almost as harrowing as losing his money. If perchance he would have the courage of his convictions, he is then not in a position to trade, his capital being tied up in bad ventures, or by this time entirely lost.

If you have ever talked with old Wall Street speculators (the majority of them, by the way, rather seedy looking fellows) you may have noticed that their conversation is almost entirely upon what they might have made, but didn't. There is always an " if " that stood in the way of their making millions; they glow with the great opportunities and wonderful possibilities of Wall Street speculation, but theirs is a tale of great opportunities lost and a direful dirge of harrowing regrets.

It is a peculiar feature of Wall Street speculation that the novice never gets his courage worked up to buy stocks until the market is right on the top, and he never concludes to sell until the market is clear on the bottom.

It is truly remarkable what accuracy a greenhorn is capable of in this direction. If you could watch one of them trade and then do just the opposite yourself, in a short time, you ought to be in a position, financially, where you would require the services of private detectives to accompany you about and protect your person from cranks and the curious.

Now what is the reason for this? Why is it that a greenhorn executes such peculiar antics, and in his

efforts to make money at the game, relieves himself
of his last dollar! Well, the novice and all outsiders,
old-timers for that matter, are dancing to the music of
the so-called " insiders," who, I can assure you, never
fiddle for nothing. Who these insiders are and how the
game is run, I will endeavor to explain.

No one is in a position to know anything about the
future course of the stock market, except those con-
nected with the large banking interests, the officers and
directors of the corporations, whose stocks and bonds
are traded in, on the New York Stock Exchange, the
pool managers or operators and the largest brokerage
houses. This constitutes the faction known as the
" insiders " or as " underground Wall Street " and
while the market is of course governed, considerably,
by general conditions, these people, through their vast
interests, are large factors in creating and forcing conditions, and they virtually control and manipulate the
game and direct the course of the market's fluctuations, as they please; or if, in any event, the market is
beyond control, they are in a position to turn quickly
with it, in advance of the public.

Since the insiders really control the market, to forecast the course of its stock fluctuations is like trying to
guess what another man is going to do, who after you
have made your guess comes around and quietly finds
out just what it is, and then to fool you, goes and
does the contrary. Now, do you think that you are a
sharp enough guesser to make money under such con-

ditions? Those of you who have tried the shell game, sometime, know how difficult it is to beat another man at his own delusive tricks; and so you will find it in Wall Street.

The position of the insiders, you will see, is peculiarly advantageous. The large New York banking interests, for example, know the true and not the reported condition of the money market, which is a great factor in stock manipulation, and they, consequently, know about what the bank statement will be each week, before it is sent out to the public.

If for the purpose of making money appear scarce and high, cash has been withdrawn from the clearing house banks and deposited in trust companies or locked up temporarily in safe deposit vaults, or sent to the interior uncalled for, or carried over to Jersey City, as is sometimes done during a " bear raid " upon the market, these people know it. If there is news of any nature, which will affect the market, they know it in advance, even before it is sent out on the news tickers, and they, of course, take advantage of their position, accordingly.

After the officers and directors of a corporation have quietly plundered it into bankruptcy, their next effort is to unload as much of its stock as possible upon the unsuspecting public, and at the very highest prices; then if for example the sworn financial statements of such a company are being padded and doctored, by skillful bookkeeping and perjury, so as to make its business appear in a prosperous condition, the insiders know it, but mind you the outside public do not; they are fed with the most glowing and optimistic reports on this company's condition and prospects, so that they will be induced to buy the stock.

The large brokerage houses may not be in quite so advantageous a position, as the other insiders, yet they know from their books and the general trend of Wall Street affairs which side of the market the public are on, who of course are to be made to lose anyway, and they know about what the position of the insiders is — both very valuable information.

The great advantage of the insiders in this game is, therefore, perfectly manifest and accounts for the reason why the " dear public," as the " lambs " or outsiders are affectionately called, are always kept on the wrong side of the market and the reason why they cut up such surprising antics. Can you wonder at it? What chance have they, but to lose, lose, always lose.

In this connection, a scheme resorted to by the president of one of the large industrial trusts, for the purpose of unloading his stock upon the public, is both interesting and illustrative. The president, from his intimate knowledge of the trust's affairs, knew that its stock must soon rapidly depreciate in market value; he, therefore, called in his brother-in-law and said to him, confidentially, " Now if you want to make some money just buy our stock, it is going to have a big advance."

So the brother-in-law bought eagerly; he not only bought but he quietly passed the word to his friends and they in turn passed it on to their friends, among whom were widows and young women school teachers. They all rushed in and bought to hold for large profits. The stock made a trifling advance, at first, after which it began to decline and kept on declining, until it had dropped about 25 per cent.

The brother-in-law then came around to the trust magnate and said, " What are you trying to do, are you trying to ruin me? I have lost $18,000 on that fine tip of yours." " O well," said the trust president, " that's all right, don't worry about such a little matter; here is a check for your $18,000, and it is mighty cheap at that, for I unloaded nearly $5,000,000 of my stock, on the little tip and at top prices. I guess the news of that big advance must have leaked out somehow."

## V.

BUT why cannot one trade in stocks on the advice of his broker, you may ask. The brokers ought to be experts in the game; they have the advantage of long experience and close proximity to the market and the large brokerage houses have the benefit of intimate business relations with the insiders.

Well, notwithstanding what the brokers may know

2

about the market situation, do not believe for a moment, that they are going to give any valuable information to their small fry customers or to the outside public, as some might be led to suppose. That wouldn't do; if the brokers gave out such information, they, for instance, could not market the stocks of the large inside interests, which might be in their hands for sale, or could not buy stocks for them, on the bottom, and would thus lose their valuable patronage.

If an insider or a manipulator of the market holds stocks that he is anxious to dispose of, because he knows that they will depreciate in market price, and he accordingly puts them into the hands of a broker to sell, the broker is expected to call attention to these stocks in his market letters, recommending them to his customers and the public as just what they should buy for an immediate advance and for large profits. The lambs at such times rush in and buy, and the insiders sell.

The business of the New York broker, you will see, is to keep the public, who confidingly pursue their advices, misled and on the wrong side of the market. The public, that good thing (to borrow an expression) must be made to continually pour into this great hopper, the glittering gold, to feed the greedy mill of Wall Street speculation, that it may grind out colossal fortunes for a few rich insiders.

Let me give you an illustration of the effect it would have upon a broker's business and upon the market generally, if he told all that he might know and gave out correct information, in his letters of advice. Suppose, for instance, some big market manipulator has run a stock, say Southern Pacific, up twenty or thirty points and has concluded that it is now about time for him to commence unloading on the '' lambs.'' This manipulator has an immense line of stock and must begin to unload early and feed it out gradually, so as not to break the price, or he is going to '' get left.'' While doing this, he must pretend to be buying; while buying 2,000 shares he will perhaps sell 5,000 shares at the same time; every scheme must be exploited, to make a market for the stock and so induce the public to come in and kindly take it off his hands before the bottom drops out.

At such times he calls in the reporters or gladly welcomes them, when they come round on their quest for news, and sets forth his alleged views on the market situation. With reasons wise and plausible, he enlarges upon the great prosperity of the country and the sound condition of business, and affirms his honest belief in the further improvement of the stock market, and especially predicts a sharp advance in the stocks which he is now ready to unload. These views are then written up by the reporters for the public to read.

Suppose, at this juncture, the manipulator gives some broker an order to sell 25,000 shares of his Southern Pacific at certain figures or for what they will bring, and the broker should tell the public, through his market letters, or should whisper around to his customers, that this heavy operator was selling Southern Pacific and that he had an order from him to dispose of 25,000 shares. If the broker did that, every one who held the stock would at once conclude that the boom was over and would rush to sell his own holdings; the crowd would fairly fall over one another to sell out first and obtain the highest price, and before the large manipulator could unload much of anything, Southern Pacific would go down like a thousand of brick. Very likely too the rest of the market would be carried down with it.

Should the market manipulator be thwarted in this manner by his broker, he would be very apt to look upon him as a " chump," and forever afterward, that broker would not be rushed much with business from this operator nor from any of the other heavy interests in the " Street."

It will be readily seen that it is the broker's mission under such circumstances to deceive and bewilder the public. It makes a market for the stocks and insures more profitable business from his rich customers, and moreover he considers it his religious duty to keep the game running " right."

It is quite evident then that one will not acquire wealth beyond the dreams of avarice, by following a broker's advice.

## VI.

PERHAPS you say, "It seems to me that the public would come to realize, after a while, what dangers beset them in Wall Street and consequently keep out of speculation; that the withdrawal of the public would cut off Wall Street's source of revenue and thus spoil this fine sport, ' such fun for the boys, but such death to the frogs.' " — No, this does not seem to be the conclusion drawn by the inexperienced. Wall Street is an institution that has been running a long time now and there are plenty of victims, coming on all the while, who seeing others go to ruin there, on every hand, yet think that *they* can beat the game — such is its peculiarly delusive and dangerous nature.

Wall Street insiders do not worry themselves over a scarcity of " lambs; " they go on the old theory, somewhat inelegantly expressed, that a " sucker," as they say, is born every minute, on a general average, and, consequently, there will always be an inexhaustible supply. This, however, seems to me a rather high average; the people universally are becoming more and more enlightened and not so gullible as they once were, and I would not be surprised if this general average has been reduced now to something like a

" sucker," born every other minute. This average, nevertheless, makes a good liberal supply and a thriving business for Wall Street.

As for the Wall Street crowd, generally, the Wall Street brokers and the insiders, who run the game, let me say, right here, by way of warning, that a ring of more consummate rascals never get together — never; and these people are the more dangerous, for the reason that they present the polished appearance of eminent respectability and fair dealing.

If a broker is engaged in carrying speculative accounts on margin, he is running what, in reality, is a gambling institution, in which one man gets another man's money for nothing. Furthermore, this is the very worst form of gambling — simply ruinous to most people who engage in it. To make in the game is worse than to lose, because it finally lures men on to lose their all, not only money, but hope, courage and capacity for honest work.

Such an occupation, from its very nature, certainly has no remarkably high moral uplift in it; but on the contrary a tendency to develop men without a conscience, and consequently you will find New York brokers, and especially Wall Street manipulators, hard and heartless, with no more conscience than a stone. Wouldn't it be foolish to expect anything else, in an open game of " dog eat dog and the Devil take the hindmost? "

If then one is going into Wall Street, as a speculator, he has to look out for Wall Street, and if he goes into the '' Street '' understanding conditions and methods as they are, that is, if he goes in to steal and should then get '' stole,'' what is he going to say or do about it anyway? But when people are first drawn into Wall Street speculation, they do not understand these matters; in fact, they generally know less than nothing about the game, because what ideas they have on the subject are all wrong, their knowledge constituting, we might say, a minus quantity; they are what is called in the '' Street '' '' swift losers '' and are certainly most innocent, easy and pitiful victims.

When we come to consider the position of the insiders in the stock market, relative to that of the outsiders, it is very evident that with the insiders, as I have said, the element of chance is practically eliminated. The insiders are so powerful and so much feared that if, for instance, one of the big '' bears '' wishes to depress the market, about all that he has to do is to say '' boo '' and down it goes — at the word everybody rushes to sell.

By making market conditions appear precisely the opposite of what they really are, the insiders keep the public on the losing side and put themselves on the winning side. This is the principal part of what is known as stock market manipulation and is accom-

plished in a hundred skillful and mysterious ways, too
dark and devious to investigate here, in detail.

In this connection, it will be understood, that you
cannot have a market where every one is of the same
opinion — sentiment must be divided — when, for instance, one wishes to sell stocks, there must be another
on hand who thinks it for his advantage to buy, and
vice versa; that makes the necessary two sides to the
market.

This sentiment in Wall Street is made to order for
the " lambs " by the insiders and fashioned to suit
their own purposes.  The newspapers are very potent
factors in accomplishing this end and are always used
by the manipulators to steer the public upon the wrong
side.  Very little financial news gets into the papers,
which will not further the interests of the insiders.
What the newspaper reporter must have, of course, is
" copy " and his pay for it; he must hand it in, at just
such a time; he has no means or opportunity of inves-
tigating the truth of what he hears and writes; he does
not have much time even to write it; so the inside
manipulators lie to the reporters, the reporters, inno-
cently, let us hope, mislead the newspapers and the
press, though doing the best it can, misleads the people.

The speculative public feed upon these lies, form
their opinions upon them, and then plunge into the
stock market, with their money, to double it, and come
out paupers.

In the end, it is true, the press arrives at the facts; but it is too late then for the speculator; he reads with empty pockets. The market has long since discounted the facts. Hence it follows that if one would get a correct idea of the stock market situation from the newspapers, he must read it from between the lines, or spell it for himself, from figures, which are often given out incorrect or in such form as to deceive. Do you wonder that the public always lose, when the newspapers are about their only source of information upon which to forecast the course of the market.

This may not be the fault of the press, because it is generally impossible to obtain the facts immediately affecting the market, so carefully are such matters kept guarded; but on this point we will refrain from mentioning certain subsidized financial sheets, published in the Wall Street district, and we will pass over those financial writers for the daily press, who are bribed by the manipulators to give such a coloring to their articles as their employers may dictate.

By the time the insiders are ready to sell their stocks, you see it is comparatively easy, through these methods, to have the public all deceived into believing that it is now just the time for them to buy if they would become rich. And on the other hand, when the insiders are ready once more to buy stocks, it is as easy to have the public again misled into thinking that now is the time for them to sell, if they would get out before the crash comes.

Wall Street speculation might be likened to a crooked game of cards. Suppose in crossing the Atlantic, on one of the great ocean liners, you fall in with some " poker sharps," who have been lying in wait for you. They have the cards all plainly marked, but in such a manner that the marks cannot be seen by you, even if suspected. Now, what chance do you think there would be for you to win, no matter how well you understand the game? As with the insiders in the stock market, these sharpers take no chances. In addition to the marked cards, suppose that you are at the disadvantage of being a greenhorn at the game, and dependent upon the other players to tell you how to play, while they are old " card sharps " and make gambling a steady occupation. Don't you think that your chances would be slimmer still, if possible? In case you won anything at all, it would be a voluntary contribution, on their part, for the purpose of inveigling you in deeper; and thus cleaning you to a finish. What folly to put up your money under such conditions.

So it is with the Wall Street game, you, inexperienced, are playing with marked cards, as it were, and are in the hands of old sharpers, who, through the press and brokers' and tipsters' letters, are actually telling you how to play into their hands. In appearance, these sharpers are very kind, dignified and respectable gentlemen, well calculated to disarm suspicion; but your chances of winning are just as propitious in Wall Street as in the poker game on the ocean steamer — the game just as respectable and the methods employed against you analogous. Consequently it is a foregone conclusion that, when a novice hands his money into a broker's office for margin, it is goodbye money and when he writes out an order for a trade in stocks, he is sending a written invitation to disaster.

Such is the nature of the Wall Street game and such are the methods of those who operate it. Is there anything more heartless or despicable? "Al." Adams, the notorious policy king, was duly exposed, properly railed at by the press and finally landed where he belongs; but infamous and pitiless as his game may have been, it was a mere bagatelle compared with the great game of the multi-millionaires in Wall Street.

## VII.

MOST of you, doubtless, have heard of " bucket shops," and perhaps some of you may have wondered to what branch of the hardware trade or to what department of the cooperage business they belong. This, however, is a kind of shop which pertains to Wall Street alone, rather than to any line of legitimate business; and what sort of an institution this is permit me to explain.

A regular broker, when he receives an order to buy
or sell stock, has it executed on the floor of the Stock
Exchange, that is, he buys the stock and has it delivered
to him to hold for his customer or in case of a short
sale, he sells the stock, then borrows and delivers it to
another broker, for the purchaser, these deliveries
being made through the Stock Exchange Clearing
House.

The proprietor of a " bucket-shop " on the contrary
does not do this; he merely enters the transaction
on his books the same as though he had really bought
or sold the stock, and he, therefore, holds no stock
for his customer.

For example, suppose you give a bucket-shop proprietor an order to buy 200 shares of a certain stock
at par, that is, for $100 a share. As the purchase
price of the 200 shares would be $20,000, you deposit
$2,000 with your so-called broker, as a ten point, or,
in other words, a 10 per cent. margin, on the pur-
chase price of the stock. Then suppose the stock de-
clines from 100 to 90, at which figure 90, the stock is
sold at the 10 per cent., or $2,000 market decline.
Since the proprietor has not bought the stock, but
merely carried the transaction on his books, he has
had nothing in his possession to depreciate in value
and no money has really been lost in the deal by any
one.

Nevertheless, the bucket-shop proprietor seizes your
$2,000, deposited with him as margin; and he also

charges you with interest on $18,000, money which you are supposed to have borrowed, as the balance over your $2,000 required to buy the $20,000 worth of stock, but which money in fact was never loaned; and he also charges you commissions for both buying and selling the stock, which he has neither bought nor sold for you.

The bucket-shop business virtually consists in transferring the customer's deposits to the credit of the bucket shop and in charging the customer commissions and interest for doing it.

It is the policy of Wall Street, that when a man is relieved of his money, he must be charged high for having it done, otherwise he might suspect that he had been robbed. After paying high for the service, the victim goes away much better satisfied and thinks that all has been done for him that could be.

This business, it will be seen, is profitable to the proprietor, when the market goes against the customer, which is generally the case. The customer does not lose any more than he would, with a regular broker, in the execution of the same orders; but the customer is placed at the disadvantage of having his so-called " broker " working against him, all the time, and watching to seize the money, which he has deposited as margin. In fact it is said that bucket-shop firms generally divide up the money, deposited with them, as soon as received, they feel so sure of it. When the market goes in favor of the customer, of course the proprietor loses; but on the whole, it makes a very profitable business, if large enough, and about a sure thing.

As these institutions all pose before the world as bankers and have the supreme assurance to style themselves, " Bankers and Brokers," in dazzling gilt letters, few of their customers ever know the difference or suspect that their orders are " bucketed " — they merely know in the end that they have been cleaned out.

Considering the manner in which the bucket-shop business is managed, one of the most pathetic situations that I know of is to see a trader, in one of these institutions, when the market runs against him, go around to the proprietor or manager of the place and ask his advice as to what he shall do, in order that he may get out of his trouble.

When the trader loses, the proprietor makes, and when the trader makes, the proprietor loses. After you are once good and safe in Hades, why not approach his Supreme Majesty and tremblingly ask him, if he will please show you a crack or a rathole, somewhere, to crawl out of — it would be as diplomatic and you would as likely escape.

Some of the regular brokers, on the New York Stock Exchange, " bucket " their small orders, such as they think are on the wrong side of the market, the same as would be done in a regular bucket-shop; that is, they bucket the orders of the lambs and their small-fry traders, who are generally wrong, and thus the broker cleans up the whole thing, margin, interest and commissions.

The broker reasons about as follows: " Here is a ' lamb,' who wants to speculate; he is going to lose, anyhow; ' a fool and his money are soon parted,' and I may as well have his money as some trader or the bucket-shop next door. Why shouldn't I work this game for all there is in it? Business is business. Since the lamb is about to be slaughtered, I may as well slaughter him and get what he will render, as my competitor across the way."

This Wall-Street moralizing would not seem so harsh, perhaps, if, under the circumstances, the broker did not quietly throw all the dust possible in his customer's eyes, to bewilder and mislead him and thus keep him on the wrong side of the market, make him lose and then say to him afterward, " I am very sorry but you did it yourself."

If I were not going to trade very heavily, and assuming that a bucket-shop firm is financially responsible, as some are, notwithstanding all that may be said against such an institution, I would much prefer it to a so-called regular brokerage house, where they " bucket " part of their orders. It is about the same old confidence game. in either place, for that matter; but as the advice of a bucket-shop proprietor would naturally be looked upon with suspicion, he keeps more quiet and does not try to confound his customers so much; he lets them work out their own destruction.

This, of course, may take a little longer than where the customer is led straight up to the precipice and pushed off; but the bucket-shop proprietor relies upon the old and very true theory, that "if you give a calf enough rope it is sure to hang itself sooner or later," and that there is no need of being in such a hurry about it.

If, however, the bucket-shop is not financially responsible, as many small ones are not, when you lose you don't get it, and then when you make you don't get it; this constitutes a kind of double twister which holds out faint hope of vast wealth; but on the contrary the prospect of a rapid depletion of your exchequer.

A New York Stock Exchange brokerage firm, doing business in the Wall Street district for many years, reaps a rich harvest in the " bucketing " business from the lambs throughout the country. The advertisements of this firm and the market letters of one of its members are published widely, in the country papers, for the purpose of attracting the attention of the unsophisticated. There can be no more lucrative and easy business than that of luring in the green-horns, gaining their confidence and taking the first crack at them. When the lambs come into the " Street," this firm receives the lion's share of their business and after their money is once put into the hands of these sharpers for margin account, they do not intend that their customers shall ever get away with a dollar of it.

No identification is required when the newcomer arrives to deposit his money, but later, if he wishes to withdraw his account and is fortunate enough to have anything on the books to withdraw, every barrier possible is put in his way. He must be identified first, now that they know him, and no one brought for the purpose is satisfactory. If the brokers can keep him a little longer they know that they are sure of his whole account.

For the purpose of getting the customer interested in the market again, possibly his attention is drawn with much skill to some market " tip," through which he is led to believe that he can make " big money." If he bites on the right side, that is on the losing side for him, his order. is " executed " with remarkable celerity, and reported as quickly as it can be set down on a book, lest he might change his mind and cancel it; but should he bite on the winning side, his order is not " executed," very likely more margin is demanded or some other effectual obstruction is raised. Needless to say, they make short work of him; and his money is very soon all transferred to the credit of the firm.

## VIII.

A WORD might be said regarding the two Stock Exchanges in New York city, the New York Stock Exchange and the Consolidated Exchange. It is generally considered more safe to do business with the New York Stock Exchange firms than with those on the " Consolidated," because by dealing with New York Stock Exchange firms you enjoy the protection of the older and stronger institution and the protection of its rules.

There may be a certain guaranty of security, from the fact that the largest brokerage firms are on the older exchange (although the largest firms are often the first to fail); but whatever there may be in this supposition, you will find that the New York Stock Exchange is an association organized for the protection of the brokers against the public; it is not even incorporated, so as to become that much amenable to the law; one broker very naturally can be expected to lie for another, as they must stand together in times of trouble, consequently, the public can expect little protection from such an institution.

Although the brokers may be perfectly square among themselves, as a matter of absolute necessity, in the execution of business on the floor of the Stock Exchange, yet if they get a chance to " do " you, you are done, and you may as well throw up both hands, and as Mark Twain said to the outlaws who " held him

up " in the western wilds, " Go through me, please,
as quickly as possible, and I will do as much for you
some time."

## IX.

I HAVE tried thus far to explain in a measure how the
" dear public " are handled by the insiders, and
relieved of their cash, or, in other words, how they
" shear the lambs; " although I must confess that in
giving an account of Wall Street methods I find it
necessary to tone down the facts considerably, in order to gain credence for what is said. Those, who
have always lived in an atmosphere removed from
Wall Street and have had no personal experience here
simply could not believe the whole truth if told; it
would be impossible for them to conceive that any
such men or methods exist.

At long intervals, however, occasions arise, when
the public are really given a little rest. On the bottom
of a " bear market," the public are so thoroughly
cleaned out and scared out that only a few remain,
holding on to their stocks; the " lambs " are about
all dead now, and those who survive are likely to
soon pass away.

As the insiders and investors hold nearly all the
stocks, picked up at panic prices, they have nothing
else to do but to turn and eat each other, and a battle
of the giants is sometimes inaugurated. Certain large

and powerful interests wish to dislodge large blocks of stock held on margin by other large speculative interests. Jealousy exists among the big men in Wall Street the same as elsewhere in the world of strife.

Since the market is about ready to be advanced twenty or thirty points, one large interest cannot bear to see another get the benefit of the advance; each wishes to gobble up the other's stock, if possible — or perhaps some corporation desires to acquire control of a certain property at rock bottom figures. So they go to work to run prices down still farther, clear below the bottom, and depress the market to such an extent that holders of these large blocks of stock will be forced out of them through exhausted margins.

This is called " gunning " for stocks, and is accomplished in various ways; for instance, by " selling the market," curtailing the money supply, calling loans, and by the large interests putting in orders to buy on a scale down when there are scarcely any other buying orders in the market. These are dangerous times for the small fellows, in case there should be any of them left carrying stocks; for if they get in the way when the " battle royal " is on, they are sure to be hurt.

Did you ever see two big bull dogs fighting furiously over a bone? Well, they remind me of the insiders fighting, or " gunning," for one another's stocks. The bull dogs growl and snarl and snap and bite at each other, and perhaps some little poodle becoming mixed in the fray gets snapped clear in two, and the big dogs in their ferocity never know it at all. They, of course, are after the bone, but it is the last of the little poodle just the same.

We take occasion to observe here that it is easy to avoid the fate of this little fellow by keeping entirely out of the *melee*. Fascinating as the game of chance may be to some natures, it can scarcely be considered wise to put your head into a lion's mouth just to see whether or not it gets snapped off.

## X.

PERHAPS the Wall Street " tipsters " would feel slighted, if I passed them by, and not wishing to have any hardness over the matter, I will introduce them for a few moments.

There are certain people in Wall Street known as " tipsters " who advertise that they can tell you how to speculate and that they will advise you every day, for a consideration, whether the market is going up or going down. This may look like a great boon, but you will find that if you take their advice and follow it very long, instead of playing the Wall Street game in New York city, you will be playing croquet at the poorhouse.

These " tipsters " issue daily letters through the mails to their customers, who pay in advance any-

where from five to twenty dollars per month for being
told how to acquire fabulous wealth. As a rule, these
fellows are dangerous frauds and sometimes unscrupulous scroundrels, who are in the employ of pools to
unload stocks upon outside speculators and investors.
The lambs send in their money to the tipsters, and
pay as usual, to be led on to ruin.

Once in a while, however, some passably honest fellow will set up in Wall Street as a " tipster," and
will try to do the best he can. Of course, he is not
an insider — far from it — nor a medium, nor a veiled
prophet, and he does not know any more about what
the insiders are doing or which way the market will
go than you do. You may be just as good a guesser
as he. If the tipster could successfully predict the
market movements, it is evident that he would not
have to bother with writing market letters every day;
he could soon sail around the Mediterranean in his
own steam yacht, having nothing to worry him.

The letters of some tipsters, let me say here by way
of parentheses, are comparatively harmless, as they
give you the priceless inside information, the gist of
which is, that if the market doesn't go up, it will go
down, and if it doesn't rain, there will probably be a
long dry time; but the shrewdest tipsters pursue this
course; they make their letters of advice both " bul-
lish " and " bearish," that is, part of the same letter
predicting an advance, and part of it predicting a decline. This leaves the speculator somewhat in doubt,

to be sure, and more or less bewildered; but the tipster is safe anyhow. No matter which way the market goes he can pick out an isolated sentence somewhere in his letters that will be all right. Afterward he can harp on this one sentence and direct the attention of his clients to it, for the purpose of showing how correct his forecasts of the market are, and then tell his customers, if they would only follow his advice they would make money.

A certain Wall Street broker writes two market letters each week; one appears in the financial column of a popular New York daily, and the other reaches the public through the mails in the form of a broker's letter, each letter being published over a different name. This broker having an eye to business and mindful of the necessity of two sides to the market, although the two letters are published at the same time, usually predicts in one that the market will advance, and in the other that the market will decline.

But, occasionally, a passably honest fellow, as I was saying, sets up as a tipster; since he guesses the best that he can he may sometimes strike it right; his customers increase and he becomes quite a little power in the " Street," on account of his following. Assuming that the tipster has any such good luck as this, when the insiders learn that he is putting his customers on the right side of the market, how they do go for him — surreptitiously, of course. If the tipster cannot be bribed, which he generally can be, with " puts " and " calls " on stocks, they employ every means in a way that he would not suspect, to " stuff him," give him points, lie to him, and thus get his clients on the wrong side of the market, and make a tool out of him for themselves. He then becomes very valuable to the insiders, for the purpose of un-loading stocks upon the public at the top, and for frightening the " lambs " out at the bottom.

To use the simplest kind of an illustration, an out-sider might as well contract to predict which way a toad will always jump, as to agree to tell which way the stock market will fluctuate. After the toad jumps the prophet can tell, but not before — just as what is called " hindsight," in Wall Street, is always good, so much better than foresight. The prophesier may think that he knows from the looks of the toad, from the direction of its nose, for instance, which way it will jump; he finds, nevertheless, that its looks are deceptive, and that just before leaping it is apt to turn suddenly and spring in the opposite direction.

It goes without saying that if the tipster were an insider his honest advice would be invaluable; but the insiders, I can assure you, have nothing to give away; you will not find them advertising to predict market movements for the " lambs," in consideration of $5 a month, correct advice on which would be worth millions. Furthermore, if they published such information, it would utterly ruin the game. Knowing the unfailing source of the advice, everybody would be of one opinion and all on the same side of the market. It is the difference of opinion, as I have explained, which makes the game possible; there must be one side to furnish the profits and the other side to rake them in.

These are some of the methods — these are some of the hidden forces — which are working constantly and insidiously toward relieving the public of that $100,000,000, and much more, year after year. Have you ever contributed anything toward that fund? If so, instead of handing the money over to these sharpers, would it not be better if you had given it to your orphan asylum or to your hospital or to your old ladies' home, or to your wife even — for wives, as you know, are more or less objects of charity? But I must not ask such aggravating questions.

Many of the public, however, have been somewhat fortunate, we might say, in their Wall Street losses, for the reason that they may now pose as philanthropists, and as generous contributors to a certain worthy charity — an unexpected distinction, to be sure, since they made their contributions without knowing it at the time, and I may add without any very generous impulses.

Who was it, if I may ask, by way of illustration, that paid for the libraries, which have been donated so liberally to various cities and towns in the United

States and Great Britain. Who, in reality, earned and contributed the money for their establishment? Was it the "Laird of Skibo Castle," or the deluded investors in every city, village and hamlet, who bought the common stock of the United States Steel Corporation, and got nothing for their money? Were not they the real contributors after all? Let us see, for, if this is the case, it will be a consolation to many.

When the United States Steel Corporation was formed, the larger steel properties in this country were sold to the big trust for twice and three times their actual value. The Carnegie Steel Company, for instance, was turned over to the trust for $100,000,000 more than the property had been offered for one year before. In reality it was being sold to the public this time, and the public were buying at the seller's own price — no questions asked, no objections raised. The public is always so " easy "— why shouldn't prices be doubled and trebled? What a temptation!

In the end the vast profits of these great iron masters, on the sale of their properties, were to be taken from the pockets of the victims who would buy the common stock of the United States Steel Corporation on the New York Stock Exchange. This, needless to say, was to be so adroitly managed that those, who were to be victimized in this way, would never suspect what was going on until it was too late.

The steel trust was to issue over half a billion dollars par value of common stock, without a dollar of assets behind it, and recommend it to the confiding as a sound investment security — more than $500,000,000 of stock, in its intrinsic value absolutely worthless, to be foisted upon the public for the purpose of catching the unwary!

This is what in Wall Street is called "High Finance," or to use a more modern term, "Morganeering."

When it comes to the last analysis, therefore, it will be found that the purchasers of this worthless stock were the real contributors of the money which founded the libraries in question, since from their pockets came the enormous profits of the donor, which grew out of this great stock-juggling swindle, enriching him and impoverishing thousands. Let us, at least, give the real contributors the satisfaction of regarding the ostensible donor as their trustee.

Who bought this stock? The small capitalist, the small tradesman, farmers, mechanics, clerks, and old women even, with a few hundred dollars laid aside to bury themselves with; this is the class of people who were "worked" through falsehood and large dividends (while the stock was being sold) to unload "Steel Common" upon. They got the pretty pictures called stock certificates, the great iron masters and financiers got their money.

Now, don't you think that these unfortunates ought to have a few library buildings, especially if they contain any books on Wall Street's financial methods?

But I presume it is safe to say that many of those, who were "fleeced" on Steel Common, have been cramped worse since for the necessities of life than they have been for fine library buildings, and that many of them could use their money, if they had it, to better advantage at home, for the purpose of keeping the wolf from the door.

Yet who shall say that the establishment of these libraries does not constitute a wise and enduring charity, and who shall say that therein the giver is not a munificent benefactor of the present and of coming generations, for whose charities the recipients should be truly thankful? No matter how vast the donor's wealth, and no matter what its sources, he might have kept it all for himself, being under no legal obligation to contribute any part of his millions to charity.

An acquaintance of mine went down to Coney Island one afternoon with a roll of bills in his pocket. Some "bunco steerers" got hold of him, and it was not over twenty minutes before he did not have a cent. But after the "bunco steerers" had appropriated all of his money, one of them said that he felt sorry to see him in such a predicament, and gave him a dollar with which to get back to the city. Upon his return he was telling me what gentlemen they were, how kind they appeared to be, and that he did not know what would have become of him if it had not been for their generosity.

What I have said thus far will give you some idea of the perils that await the adventurer in Wall Street. But the public never learn how to keep out of danger in stock speculation, and never can, for as soon as they have one trick well mastered a new one is sprung upon them, which no one outside the shrewd sharpers of Wall Street's inner circle would have the assurance or the ingenuity to invent.

To the inexperienced Wall Street is ever an alluring light, toward which men seem drawn by some peculiar power. Continually the moths keep flying into the flame, until their wings are scorched off and their charred carcasses fall at the foot of the candle with swarms of the other dead.

## PART II — ITS TRAGEDIES.

## XI.

NOW let me give you one little instance, showing how people are drawn unawares into stock speculation and financially ruined. A particular case will perhaps give a clearer understanding of Wall Street methods and present a more vivid picture of the speculator's life than any generalizations that I could make.

In a small town, situated in the State of Connecticut, a country merchant had been doing business for forty years. He was sixty years old now, and as the result of a lifetime of patient toil and careful economy he had accumulated what in those parts was a considerable fortune. As his income was sufficient for himself and his wife to live upon very comfortably, and as his health had partially failed he concluded to dispose of his business and retire.

A wealthy farmer in the neighborhood, having a son not in love with agriculture, wished to establish him in the mercantile trade, and when he heard that old man Brown wanted to sell his business he bought him out, store, stock, good will and all; he took the property at a fair price and paid for it in full. The old merchant always kept a large bank account, as he bought his goods for cash, and when he looked at his bank-book, after depositing the farmer's check, he had good reason to feel quite satisfied and happy. All his assets were reduced to money now, and, of course, he was looking for trouble, and trouble had all eyes peeled looking for him. In cases of this kind the parties generally meet before long and arrange for an interview.

When a man, who has devoted his life to one kind of business, finally sells out and converts his property into cash he is always an easy prey for swindling schemers. He thoroughly understands the business in which he spent his life, and, therefore, made money at it, but when he comes to handling his slippery cash in other lines, especially in those of a speculative nature, my observation has been that he nearly always gets cleaned out; and if he goes into Wall Street it seems that the more careful and conservative a business man he has always been the more he will lose his head here.

But let us watch this old merchant and see him double his money. For years he has had his eye on the market for dry goods and groceries and for produce; he tried to buy his goods when the market was low, and sell his produce taken in barter when the market was high. This he generally did, and he thought he was a pretty sharp old duck at it, as in fact he really was. In watching the other markets

his attention had now and then been drawn to the
Wall Street stock market, and he thought that, if he
ever had a good chance, he would like to take a crack
at it sometime.

He always had understood that what one required
to make money in Wall Street was capital — that
money makes money there, and he had the capital now.
Then it would be such an easy and such a pleasant
occupation; he couldn't stand on his feet the way he
used to all day in the store; but he could sit in the
easy chairs of a broker's office and watch the stock
market quotations all right.  He knew that he would
like the business, and he thought it just about excit-
ing enough to be interesting.

His wife, from what little she had heard concerning
stock speculation, was somewhat wary at first, when
her husband began to talk of going into Wall Street;
but the old man said that he didn't see any great
difference between buying 100 shares of stock at 90 and
selling them at 110, and buying so many sacks of flour
at wholesale and selling them out for a profit at
retail, except that it was a mighty sight less work to
buy and sell the stock than it was the flour and ten
times more money in it — anyway, " nothing ventured
nothing gained."

The old man did not realize it, but he imbibed these
ideas from reading certain books and pamphlets,
which brokers are continually sending out through the

mails for the purpose of inveigling the public into Wall Street; and in this kind of literature, brokers, very naturally, make a special effort to veneer their gambling game with the appearance of a respectable business. If they can get people to reading these little books, they know from experience that, sooner or later, the readers will become interested in Wall Street, and come to be offered up, as it were a burnt offering, upon its altar of avarice and greed.

This reasoning of the old gentleman did look rather plausible, and as he was not going in very heavy, anyhow, his wife said that if he thought money could be made so easily down there in Wall Street, he better go along and make some.

It was as wise to say this as anything else, for when a man once gets the speculative Wall Street fever, and is smitten with the mad desire to lose his money in the quickest way possible, it is useless to advise him against it, nothing will stop him — you might as well advise a person stricken with the typhoid to reduce his temperature from one hundred and four degrees Fahrenheit down to ninety-eight and one-half — it would have the same effect.

So the old man takes a good-sized New York draft from his account at the bank, sets out for the Metropolis and deposits his money with a responsible Wall Street broker for margin account.

4

Of course, at the time this old merchant is attracted
by the stock market it is toward the end of a " bull
campaign," when stocks are selling near the top and
are about ready to turn downward. In fact, it is exceedingly seldom that a novice is drawn into Wall
Street when the market is around the bottom. In any
event, if he should come in and want to buy stocks at
such a time, the brokers would scare him out of his
wits. It is always during the loud bull chorus and
the grand hurrah, on the last end of a boom, that the
" lambs " are called in to be fleeced.

As we have seen, when the market is around the
top, every lie and every wile of which the human mind
could be capable is employed by the insiders, for the
purpose of inducing the public to buy their stocks;
but after a quick manipulated decline and the market
begins to touch bottom the insiders quietly pick up
the stocks again.

At these times the lambs and the small fry, if they
want to buy on margin, are told by the brokers that
the market looks like going lower, and on account of
the condition of the money market, or for some other
plausible reason, they can only buy stocks for cash,
that is, outright and not on margin. This course
serves to keep the public out of the market just when
they should buy. When stocks were selling 20 or 30
per cent. higher, brokers were perfectly willing to

carry all one could hold on a five or ten point margin, and they thought it perfectly safe at that, but now when stocks are down say thirty points and about to advance, they do not think it safe for the lambs to buy on a margin.

The fact is, the brokers, on these occasions of unusual opportunity, very likely when money is scarce and high, want their cash and credit to buy stocks for themselves and for a few of their favored customers and friends. They are not employing their money and credit now for the benefit of the small traders — the chances are too good; but wait a while until the market makes a good sharp advance, and the same brokers will be ready again on the top to carry on margin all the stocks that the public wish to buy. They know that it is only a short interval before the money put into their hands for margin account will be confiscated into their own pockets, or appropriated in the interests of the insiders. This is the policy pursued by most of the New York Stock Exchange brokers.

After a quick manipulated decline, to which we have just referred, the conditions, of course, are different from those prevailing after a period of prolonged and steady liquidation, like that of 1902–1903. In the latter case, when such thorough liquidation has been forced, it is necessary for a long wait before the insiders manipulate the market anew, in order to give the general public ample time to recuperate from their overwhelming losses, bury the suicides, console the broken-hearted, and accumulate more money in the channels of honest industry; meanwhile the Wall Street magnates are enjoying the proceeds of their last *coup* from the stock market, basking in the sunshine of the Riviera, cruising along the Mediterranean, reposing beneath Italian skies, and hobnobbing with princes in the castles of Europe. But after due time, when the common people become worth the game, some new scheme is devised by Wall Street to lure the public into the stock market once more and clean them out again. And so the good work goes on.

But we will return now to our rural merchant. His broker had no more than caught sight of him, when he was recognized as one of the " lambs," and as he has deposited quite a large sum for margin account, his kind friend and adviser, the broker, tries to make an estimate of how much more money the old man has back to be relieved of, and then advises him to buy, buy, buy.

The broker knows that his customer, being inexperienced, would not sell stocks short for a decline, as he should at this time, even if he urged him to — he would not understand the transaction. Moreover, since prices appear to be near the top, the broker has stocks himself for sale, as well as orders from old customers to sell their holdings at top-notch figures, and he is interested in making a market for them.

More than likely, however, his broker advises him
to buy, then " buckets " his orders and takes the
chances; but the chances are very few in such a case
if the broker can get his customer to give purchasing
orders at inflated prices, when the market is at a dizzy
height.

Our rural friend, having now become a little more
accustomed to the turmoil down in Wall Street, and
having got his sand up on good advice and encourage-
ment from his broker, sails in and buys for a starter
200 shares of St. Paul, that is 200 shares of the Chi-
cago, Milwaukee & St. Paul R. R., a speculative
favorite in Wall Street. Everything is more or less
lively along toward the end of a " bull campaign,"
especially St. Paul stock, which made an advance of
nearly three points the same day that he bought it, and
netted a profit on the 200 shares of over $500.

This set the old man nearly crazy. When he compared such a method of making money to selling salt
mackerel and drawing thick molasses in cold weather,
and then waiting for the pay until his customers sold
their steers or butchered their hogs — when he made
these comparisons he could not help reflecting upon
what a fool he had been during all his past life. He
determined now to get immensely rich; he had the
capital to do it and he was not going to be very long
about it either.

As St. Paul seemed to be a good jumper, the next

day he bought 500 shares more. After he bought the
stock it sagged a little, and he wondered what was the
matter, but between 2 and 3 p. m. the market rallied
and St. Paul closed about a point and a half higher
than where he bought it, and he stood, on the books
of the brokers, something like $1,200 ahead for the
two days.

He was crazier than ever now. All the tipsters in
Wall Street said that the market was going a great
deal higher, and stated the prices to which the more
active stocks would advance. Accordingly, he began
to figure out how heavy a burden his margin account,
including profits, would carry, and the next day he
loaded up with all the stocks that his funds would
hold on a safe ten-point margin.

Along in the afternoon of the same day the market
began to drop off easily, money was loaning at 10 per
cent. on call, and it was reported that the National
City Bank had been calling loans, which was the case.
The Standard Oil crowd, who control the National
City Bank and various other Wall Street banks, and
who, by the way, virtually run the stock market to
suit themselves, having completed the sale of their
speculative holdings, and, moreover, having sold stocks
short (that is without having them), were now anxious
to put the market down as far as possible, buy in their
short sales at low prices, and accumulate stocks for
another advance.

Aided by the inflated condition of the market, which they had previously fostered and encouraged to sell out on, they proceed to force prices down, among other methods by making money scarce and high and by setting afloat direful and alarming rumors.

The allied Standard Oil banks and their correspondents throughout the country are said to control nearly one-half of the money in the United States, and in times of inflation, the National City Bank alone (to say nothing of the others) has anywhere from one hundred and forty to one hundred and fifty million dollars out in loans, a considerable part of this amount, loaned in Wall Street " on call," and upon securities, as collateral, which are dealt in by speculators on the New York Stock Exchange.

You can readily see what a power these banks are to the Standard Oil people in manipulating the market either up or down. Since they hold so many loans in their various banks, upon stocks carried on margin, the business of brokers and the large operators and their speculative position is an open book to these great manipulators, and they consequently know just when, where and how to strike a blow of death to the market.

The National City Bank accordingly begins to call loans, right and left, which precipitates upon the market thousands of shares of stock, held by this bank as collateral. Since borrowers are unable to obtain accommodations elsewhere, their certificates of stock, put up as collateral security for loans, are sold at the market. Other banks are soon compelled to pursue the same course in order to protect their loans upon rapidly depreciating collateral, which brokers and other borrowers are unable to keep margined up to bank requirements. Frightened holders of stocks begin to unload and " old-timers " to sell short; and the market is soon deluged with securities, nearly every one wild to sell and few wishing to buy.

The Standard Oil crowd thus ultimately succeed in precipitating a panic, Wall Street failures and general demoralization and disaster, shaking the financial world of both hemispheres to its remotest corners. In this way they confiscate the money of the public into their own capacious pockets, already so generously filled.

## XII.

THIS was a phase of the speculative situation which the old merchant little understood; he thought that the market must soon recover, and as general business was still in a flourishing condition, he looked for an advance in stocks to prices still higher than they had yet reached. He did not know that Wall Street anticipates and discounts long in advance all the prosperity in sight, even through the most powerful houses. He did not know that a burst of glory in the business world is a signal for the insiders in the stock market to unload upon an eager public, and then start the manipulation of decline and panic.

The fifth day after being launched upon this, at first smooth sea of speculation, the old man found the waters becoming exceedingly rough and dangerous. The market kept on sagging; it had a good start now and by night his profits were all wiped out and he had lost about $5,000 besides.

As a merchant, he had not been accustomed to losing money that fast and it began to start the cold sweat upon his brow; he stood around dazed and looked on, while his hard-earned money was melting away by the thousands. His kind friend the broker did not seem to be much in evidence at this juncture; he did not see him around anywhere to advise what he should do. The old man concluded, however, to hang on to his stocks until the market would turn in his favor, and in that way not lose anything after all.

The situation in Wall Street was now beginning to look exceedingly dismal, where only a few days before everything appeared so roseate. All the bad news seemed to have been dammed back for months and let out at this time systematically. The next day he was out about $10,000 more, and was called by his broker for additional margin at once; so in order to save what money he had in, and see the thing through, he gave the broker a check for all that he had left in his bank up in Connecticut.

Down, down, down, the stocks tumbled; with dark, haggard faces speculators pace the floor of brokers' offices, in all the anxieties of hell, with trembling hands they hold the ticker tape, which tells the sad story, and see the savings of a life-time swept from their grasp — yonder sits a man glaring at the floor, half-crazed, contemplating suicide — men see themselves irretrievably ruined, and drop dead at the ticker! But how the Standard Oil people and other insiders are now making money out of these unfortunates on their short sales; and what bargains they are picking up in cheap stocks, forced from the hands of weak holders, and that of course is enough — no gold mine on earth ever turned out profits with such rapidity.

Presently the old merchant was almost paralyzed by another call for additional margin. If he failed to com- ply at once his stocks would be closed out, and he would lose everything. His own resources had become en- tirely exhausted; but obtaining the indorsement of a friend, he borrowed some money at his country bank, and poured that also into the howling vortex. Then came a little rally; the market was getting near the bottom, but at last it took another slide down and plunged the old man to his financial ruin.

After this the market rallied and started on its course upward. Although the old merchant had a small margin on his account, at the lowest quotations reached on the decline, nevertheless his broker closed him out, right on the bottom and just as the market was turning for a prolonged advance. At these opportune times, when stocks are depressed far below their intrinsic value, the insiders are particularly anxious to take over the cheap stocks of the " lambs," especially after the latter have brought their last dollar into Wall Street for the purpose of carrying their accounts through a decline. It keeps this money in the " Street " and likewise leaves the " come-ons " without any stocks and without any hope of recovering their money. More greenhorns and more margins are now in order — and thus thrives Wall Street.

The way the old fellow took on in the broker's office when he learned that he had been sold out and hopelessly ruined was the source of considerable sport with the broker and his clerks for several days afterward.

At first, when he complained about his misfortune, the broker and his office manager gave him the " hoarse laugh," or what is sometimes called the " grand haha; " but when they saw how agitated he was, they thought that perhaps it would be better policy to handle him differently; so they changed their tactics a little and slapped him on the back and said, "Awfully sorry, old man, awfully sorry; but we just had to close you out, you know; if you had put up more margin, we would have carried you through."

The facts of the case are, most likely, that they had " bucketed " his orders or disposed of his stocks soon after the decline began; but, notwithstanding this, had kept him handing in money to " margin down his account," and they were now alarmed, when the market was apparently near the bottom, lest he might put up a large margin and thus give them no good chance to scoop him.

Needless to say, now that the victim had been plundered of his last dollar and more (for he was in debt to his bank), he was of no further use to the broker, in fact, like the ruined player at Monte Carlo, a bad advertisement.

At Monte Carlo, however, when a player loses his all, it is the humane custom of the establishment to provide him with sufficient money for his expenses home; but not so in Wall Street — the victim can walk home or blow his brains out or jump from the top of a twenty-story building, nobody cares. Accordingly, the chief concern of the broker, in this case, was to get rid of the old man, as quietly and gracefully as possible. But this little matter was skillfully and successfully managed, since the broker had become a trained expert in this line through long practice.

That night, away from the noise of the street, in the quiet of his little room at the hotel, the old man sits, with his face in his hands, and thinks it all over again. The full realization of his disaster now begins to set-

tle down upon him. Ruined! ruined! worse than
ruined, and sixty years old! For forty years, he and
his faithful wife had toiled and saved; he never took
a vacation, he never had any time or thought that he
could afford to attend a theater or a lecture. His wife
did her own work and helped in the store. He not
only worked all day, but posted books half the night.
Competition was keen and profits were small, which,
with the loss of a few bad accounts every year, made
the process of accumulating a fortune somewhat slow,
but he was industrious, careful and close; he had allowed himself few pleasures and little recreation; he
never thought that he had time to rest, and in acting
as proprietor, general manager, buyer, salesman and
bookkeeper in his store, he was too tired even for pleasure when his work was over.

Most everything for which life is worth living, except work, he had crowded out of his existence. He
had always been getting ready to enjoy himself when
he had saved so much money. He had always enter-
tained the laudable ambition of making his old age and
that of his wife comfortable and free from care and
worry. This ambition he had fully realized when he
was drawn into Wall Street. Could he go through it
all again and begin over where he started, forty years
ago? could he go home now and tell his wife? could he
go back and face the community and his debt at the
bank, without a dollar? No! No! sick, disheartened,

half insane, he clutches his revolver and blows his brains out.

Now who murdered that man? The scoundrels who manipulated the Wall Street game drew him into it and got his money. They are really the ones who murdered him, as well as thousands of others, who have suffered the same deplorable fate; these scoundrels are morally, if not legally, responsible. That is the way to become immensely rich and do it quick — kill people for their money! But do it systematically and within the law, mind that you do it indirectly and within the law. This please recognize as the severest irony, on my part; but I want to give you a little idea of the methods employed in Wall Street.

The suicides which follow in the wake of stock market manipulation are something appalling, and notwithstanding the efforts of certain pious Wall Street magnates to throw an odor of sanctity over Wall Street and lead the public to believe that it is a divine institution, few I think are as yet convinced that driving men to suicide can be regarded as a highly moral occupation, no matter how indirect the methods employed, no matter how religious those engaged in it, or how profitable the business.

## XIII.

THE next morning the newspapers made slight mention of the old merchant's death, something as follows: "Suicide of wealthy country merchant, while temporarily insane, no other cause known for the deed, as he had no family or financial troubles." He was not of much account anyway in a great city like New York; and since the brokers hushed the little matter up as much as possible lest it might hurt business, this is the last that the public ever heard about the incident — and Wall Street goes on, luring in more victims, ruining more lives, wrecking more homes, spreading more misery and driving more men to insanity and death.

Although the financial kings of Wall Street already possess hundreds of millions of dollars, although among their number are men, whose individual wealth is greater than the assessed valuation of some whole States, yet so great is their sordid greed that none of them hesitate at methods of this kind for a single instant — provided they can clutch more money! more money!

Now don't you think that Wall Street speculation is a wicked game, a gigantic robbery, rather than a legitimate business, and don't you think that such a game ought to be stopped?

I say that speculation in stocks on a margin should be constituted a crime under the law, as it is in reality. It fosters a ring of idle gamblers, parasites upon society, who prey upon the fortunes of the honest and industrious; such people are a menace to the legitimate business interests of the country and an element of danger to the republic.

Petit larceny is promptly punished, as it should be; but why indorse grand larceny and let the big thieves go free? We must confess that the man who commits petit larceny generally has neither influence nor money, and that when this fact comes to light the vigor with which he is pounced upon is truly pitiful; we must likewise acknowledge that the big thieves have such fabulous wealth as would make Crœsus feel poor; but, notwithstanding this, under what code of morals or under what true system of jurisprudence should the petty pilferers be punished, and the wholesale robbers allowed to fatten and flourish, immune from restraint and punishment under the law?

If robbery is only committed on a scale sufficiently grand and colossal, the majesty of the law is appalled; if a few smooth Wall Street gentlemen defraud the public out of their honestly acquired wealth and take it by the scores of millions, Justice stands by paralyzed and helpless, in the presence of a crime of such stupendous proportions, as to be outside the scope and contemplation of the law — but with what heavy hands she lays hold of the man who steals a chicken! For these absurdities and inconsistencies, in our jurisprudence, let us hope that the slow growth of the law will ultimately evolve effectual remedies.

Members of Congress and of other legislative bodies, as well as Presidents of the United States, if in league with market manipulators and speculating in Wall Street, should be compelled by law to forfeit the office, which they thus prostitute to private gain. The speculating legislator or other government official employs his power, not for the welfare of his constituency or the country at large, but merely for his own private pocket and without the slightest regard for the peoples' interests, which he is employed to protect. Such are Wall Street's statesmen and patriots, of which we have had an example in at least one President.

Furthermore, should not the amount of wealth which one man shall be allowed to roll up, under some unusual advantage, be regulated by law, and the dangerous and disturbing billionaire rendered impossible? There is of course a difference of opinion on this question, some political economists maintaining that if an individual were limited in his acquisitions, to say fifty million dollars, instead of to a possible billion, it would work complete stagnation and paralysis to personal ambition and personal enterprise. I would not assume to be an authority on this point; but I think that the *consensus* of opinion is, that it can scarcely be safe for one man, like our greatest millionaire, to hold so much money power in this Republic, that all the rest of the financial world simply does not dare to oppose him, no matter how predatory or piratical his ambitions; to oppose whom means absolute ruin and annihilation; that it can scarcely be consistent with the general welfare for one man to become so powerful that he may own Legislatures and benches of judges, and even presume to dictate to the Senate of the United States.

What other influence is there, in this country, let me ask, that is breeding with so great rapidity, the lamentable spirit of socialism and anarchy?

## XIV.

LET us return now for a moment to the old lady, the merchant's wife. It is a deplorable fact, that, when the head of a household is ruined financially, his family, through no fault of theirs, must often suffer more than he. I will not attempt to depict the old lady's feelings when she learned the true situation — a widow and nearly destitute in her old age.

After the funeral is over, she tries to think what she can do. Her home even was sold, for that was a part of the store property and went with it. Years ago, in the distribution of her father's estate, the farm which he had left was sold and the proceeds divided among seven or eight children, and she had received from that source a small sum of money. This she had kept on interest, always adding the increase to the principal until it had amounted to five or six hundred dollars. This money, heretofore almost forgotten, is now her only resource. Out of it she paid the funeral expenses and then took what remained and turned it over to an old ladies' home. It at least might buy her a place to die.

Upon receiving notice of her admission to the home, she sets out for the place where she is to pass her last sad and lonely years. Feebly and tearfully she climbs the long steps and presents herself at the office of the institution. The authorities are sorry that they can give her no better accommodations; but it is the best that they can do. She will be satisfied with any-thing, she says; then she follows an attendant down a long oil-cloth covered hall, up two flights of stairs, down another long narrow hall to room 67, a little cell-like apartment, with one north window. The door is un-locked for her, she steps slowly in and closes it. The room is furnished with two chairs, a dresser and a white cot bed. She takes off her cloak and lays it on a chair, puts her long crepe veil thoughtfully on the dresser, contemplates the bare walls, so suggestive of her desolation, then falls upon her knees beside her little cot and sobs the hot tears of loneliness and despair.

But what became of the money of these old people and that of others who lost in the same way? Where is it? This money has not been destroyed; it has merely changed hands, without an equivalent being given. But who got it? I will tell you. Through the intricacies of the game, this money has passed into the hands of the great capitalists of Wall Street, never to return to those who, with a life-time of toil, honestly earned it. What will become of it? The greater portion of it, doubtless, will remain in the strong boxes of those whose iron grasp now holds it. But let us throw the most favorable light possible upon the situation. As it is easy to be generous with other people's money, part of this old merchant's fortune, together with a tithe from much more made in the same way, may sometime constitute a gift, which one of these great capitalists turns over, with a loud report, to a university or a theological seminary or to some other charity. He hands it over, as a sort of conscience fund, to give him a fresh start in more Wall Street enterprise of the same kind, and the world looks on and says, " This is indeed true charity, God bless the philanthropist! "

Perhaps, that very night, while the old lady was sobbing beside her little cot, the fortune which she and her husband had toiled so long and hard to earn, flashed in

a tiara of diamonds from the head of a rich broker's
wife at the opening night of the Metropolitan Grand
Opera — diamonds, wondrously beautiful, dazzlingly
brilliant, crystalized human tears. If you could go
around that row of parterre boxes and write the his-
tory of all those pearls and all those rubies and all
those diamonds, it would compose a tragedy that would
make your heart bleed.

What an enchanting scene is the opening night of
the Metropolitan Grand Opera! The rarest gems of
earth dance in ten thousand lights; beautiful women,
the soft perfume of exotic flowers and the voluptuous
swell of grand music thrill the soul — verily, '' the cup
run th over,'' and all hearts seem filled with every
joy. But how can we help reflecting upon what a contrast is this brilliant scene to that in the little room at
the old ladies' home — yet what do these people care
about this desolate widow and their thousands of other
victims? Absolutely nothing — in fact their victims,
if thought of at all, are the subject of sarcasm and jest;
they are the '' lambs that got fleeced.''

There must not be any sentiment in business, is their
doctrine — it interferes. If you would make millions,
business must be utterly heartless, utterly heartless!
Those terse aphorisms, '' Business is business '' and
'' Do others or they will do you '' receive much admi-
ration here, as maxims both of high moral worth and of

great practical utility; but such sentiments as "A good
name is rather to be chosen than great riches, and
loving favor rather than silver and gold," have been
crossed out and labeled " back numbers " and " no
good in Wall Street."

If there is any doctrine which this class of people
dotes on, it is that of " the survival of the fittest." Ap-
plicable as this doctrine is, in the world of strife, its
application here seems somewhat perverted and para-
doxical since, in Wall Street, the most consummate
trickster and the most heartless scoundrel with the big-
gest pile of dollars is the fittest and he is the one who
does the surviving. And then the following is much re-
lied on in justification of Wall Street methods: " For
whosoever hath, to him shall be given, and he shall have
more abundance: but whosoever hath not, from him
shall be taken away, even that he hath." This passage,
of course, refers to the acquisition of more knowledge
of the truth, as the theologians tell us; but the money
kings of Wall Street like to give its interpretation a little twist in their favor, and say that it refers to the acquisition of more greenbacks, by the big fellows from
the little ones. In fact, this class of people appear to
hold the opinion that if they would succeed in anything
questionable or crooked, there is nothing like misin-
terpreting the Scriptures their own way, so as to apparently justify them in their rascality before the
public.

This is a little of Wall Street theology and Wall Street business ethics. Do you wonder that such theologians could insert about eight hundred million dollars of wind into the United States Steel Trust and something like forty million dollars more into the United States Shipbuilding Trust, and then sell it to the public without a twinge?

Coming from Wall Street, I hope that I shall not be misunderstood as proselyting for this kind of a creed — far from it — nor for any particular creed, being engaged in legal instead of evangelistic work. I thought, nevertheless, that I should merely touch upon the convenient theology and ethics of Wall Street, as well as upon its other phases, especially since those, who have made the most conspicuous successes here have been particular to pose before the public as eminent churchmen. The connection of such men with churches, however, has done more to spread infidelity and cast reflection and ridicule upon the good cause of the church than almost anything else.

The success of this class of gamblers has an influence for evil upon the business world that is little realized, success through their methods being a contradiction to the good old business maxim that "Honesty is the best policy" and a travesty upon it. The moral law seems perverted here. Wrong appears right and right wrong. Young men look down from the galleries and far off corners of that great Opera House and say, "If you would make millions, that is the way, speculation, gambling, rascality, anything but honest work. The rascal is exalted and his victim disgraced."

Since these great Wall Street magnates are continually kept before the public, as shining examples of success for the youth to emulate, is it any wonder that the business world is becoming more and more shrewd, dishonest and unscrupulous? The young man says to himself, when imitating the great financiers and capitalists of our day, "Can I be sufficiently dishonest and at the same time sufficiently pious to succeed in life; can I be just dishonest enough to graze State prison, but at the same time keep out through bribery, perjury and hypocrisy?"

The effect of this influence crops out in all kinds of so-called "hot air" and "get rich quick" swindles, 520 per cent. Miller games, discretionary pool frauds, turf investment companies, etc., etc., which relieve the confiding public of anywhere from ten to twenty millions of cold cash at one sweep.

## XV.

THE experience of this Connecticut merchant, which I have given you, is only one little case among thousands. Think of the misery, think of the tears, think of the disgrace and remorse which the tremendous losses of the public to these Wall Street sharpers, year after year, certainly entails. Who can realize it?

The massive iron doors of State prison clank behind a man, from some responsible and trusted position of business life; in an hour of temptation, he was drawn into Wall Street speculation, with trust funds. He lost. The court and jury say he is guilty of grand larceny. He has lost the money bequeathed into his charge by a father, for the support and education of several young children. They are now left destitute. When he reflects upon what he has done, through this alone as punishment, he suffers all the torments of the damned; but in addition to this, he must go to prison and wear the stripes, for ten long weary years. Dazed, they lead him from the courtroom, all he hears is the heart breaks of his wife and innocent children, disgraced by him forever. Into a solitude worse than death they lead him and clank behind the doors of his eternal doom.

Such is his fate; but what about the Wall Street sharpers who drew him into this trouble and who now have the money of these children, safely deposited, to their already stupendous bank accounts — what about them? Oh, they are all right; they pose as financiers, great " captains of industry," and as men of remarkable genius in the business world.

The general public do not understand and the people

who acquire their wealth in this manner take every
precaution possible that the public shall not understand; sometimes they endow churches and teach Bible
classes, as a blind, or pass the Sacrament of the Lord's
Supper at the celebration of Holy Communion.

This renders their course of crime easy and profitable and enables them at the same time to be looked
upon by those who do not know them and their methods as highly respected citizens and Christian gentlemen; but notwithstanding what their appearance may
be before the public, I have often wondered, when they
are teaching Sunday school and passing the Sacrament, what kind of an appearance they are making
before God, the God of love for all mankind, the God
of the fatherless.

The church is a strong fortress behind which such
high up rascals like to intrench themselves, in whom
the church is deceived and for whose membership,
therefore, it is not responsible, unless the church know-
ingly fosters such people and contends for them, as is
sometimes the case, because they always pay heavily
for their protection.  They can afford to; there is
money in it.

## XVI.

SO much for Wall Street and its woes, its tricks and
its tragedies, its heartlessness and its hypocrisy;
and now will you permit me to give a word of advice?

If you are inexperienced in Wall Street methods and contemplate going into that maelstrom of speculation, take your money, five, ten, twenty, or thirty thousand dollars or whatever you may anticipate venturing with, have it all stacked up in nice new bills, put it into your grip and go right direct with it to some of the great Wall Street financiers, and say " Here, Mister, is my $30,000, in good money; it is a large share of what I possess, but it is yours now, take it quick. I thought of using it as margin in Wall Street speculation, but I have concluded that you will get it anyway in the end, and you can have it now; you might just as well take it first as last, and a great deal better; it will save me much time and worry, many a wrinkle and many a grey hair and I will go right back home and give my attention to my business, before it is ruined, for I can't keep my mind on Wall Street and on my business too."

To hand over money in that prodigal manner may seem, on first consideration, manifestly rash and foolish; but if you must do either the one or the other, go into Wall Street speculation or hand the money over, the latter is altogether the better course. It will save burning out your soul in the protracted fires of suspense, anxiety and worry; it will save your health; it will save you from shattered nerves and from shattered brain; it will save you from a physical and mental condition incapacitated for honest business or professional life; it will save losing faith in your fellow man, and in your God.

There is, of course, a glamor about the possibility of making a hundred dollars in a minute, but that possibility is the siren's silver voice, that will likely lure you on to the rocks of ruin.

One would almost think that King Solomon must have had some experience in Wall Street speculation and then sat down and wrote in his proverbs as follows: " He that hasteneth to be rich hath an evil eye, and considereth not that poverty shall come upon him." If young men will take that advice, keep out of Wall Street that " hasteneth to be rich," and go to work at something honest and useful and stick to it, they will be successful and happy and " poverty shall not come upon them."

He who aspires to go through this life the easiest is almost sure to go through the hardest and finally come to a wretched and abandoned old age. What a contrast between the old age of the man who brings to the evening of life the fruits of honest industry and the satisfaction of life-long usefulness to his fellow men, and the old age of the insane gambler who brings in his bony, trembling hands nothing but the semblance of a wasted life.

Will you picture to yourself a deep and dark canyon; below are jagged rocks and a great river; 1,000 feet above, the brow of the canyon projects over the rocks and the river. Not far from the edge of this precipice a man stands; he is blindfolded and groping in the darkness. He does not realize his danger — the river is so far below that he cannot hear it. He may wander away from this yawning chasm, but not likely; and even if he would, an enemy in whose power he is stands close by, watching to turn him in the opposite direction. Moreover, the slippery rock beneath his feet slopes toward the edge of the precipice, and blindfolded, he naturally will drift in the course of the least resistance. Nearer and nearer, he gropes toward the edge. Now we see him stand on the very brink. One more step, whispers his enemy, and you are safe. He takes it — when down, down, down to death and destruction he plunges upon the sharp and jagged rocks, below.

This is the position of the speculator in Wall Street. Can you afford to take the chances of that perilous position? If so, then to Wall Street, with money, mind, body and soul, and there take your chance on life and death, your chance on Heaven and Hell.

-

Lightning Source UK Ltd.
Milton Keynes UK
UKOW04f1344020215

245509UK00001B/81/P